DON'T TELL ME

by

RICHARD J. MULLIN

MOODY PRESS

CHICAGO

Contents

© 1976 by
THE MOODY BIBLE INSTITUTE
OF CHICAGO

ISBN: 0-8024-1781-7

Which One Is False?

Some Bible facts are so familiar that we think they couldn't be mistaken. But mixed with false items, we begin to wonder which one is right. You'll find it fun as you quiz your group on these mixed-up Bible facts. The idea is to pick out the fact which is not right, from the three items given. The quiz may be used with large or small groups or at informal services at church, the opening Sunday school assembly, etc. Sides may be chosen and a score kept.

1. Three of the disciples were Peter, Luke, and Andrew. (Luke was not—Matthew 10:1-4)
2. Some of the towns in Galilee were Nazareth, Capernaum, and Bethlehem. (Bethlehem was in Judea—Matthew 2:6)
3. Seas mentioned in the Bible are the Red Sea, the Tarsus Sea, and the Sea of Galilee. (Tarsus was a city, not a sea—Acts 9:11)
4. The sign on the cross of Jesus Christ was written in Aramaic, Greek, and Hebrew. (Not in Aramaic—Luke 23:38)
5. The Sea of Galilee was also known as the Sea of Tiberias, the Lake of Gennesaret, and the Great Sea. (Not called the Great Sea—Luke 5:1; John 6:1)
6. The three disciples with Jesus in the Garden of Gethsemane were Paul, Peter, and John. (Paul was not—Matthew 26:37)
7. The three regions in Palestine were Galilee, Judea, and Syria. (Not Syria, but Samaria—John 4:4)
8. The tribes of Israel included Reuben, Judah, and Gideon. (Not Gideon; he was a judge—Judges 6:11; Revelation 7:5-8)

9. Some of the judges in Israel were Deborah, Samson, and Saul. (Not Saul; he was a king—1 Samuel 11:21-24)

10. Some of the minor prophets of the Bible are Joel, Amos, and Hezekiah. (Hezekiah was not a prophet, but a king—Isaiah 37:1)

11. The fruit of the Spirit is given as love, joy, and hope. (Hope is not listed—Galatians 5:22-23)

12. The first three kings of Israel were Samuel, Saul, and Solomon. (Samuel was a judge, not a king—1 Samuel 7:15)

13. Letters to the churches in Asia Minor were to Philadelphia, Philemon, and Laodicea, recorded in Revelation 2 and 3. (Not Philemon; he was a man, not a city—Philemon 1)

14. Paul's companions on his journeys were James, Luke, and Silas. (James was not; he was slain—Acts 12:2)

15. Pillars in the early church were Tarsus, Peter, and James. (Not Tarsus; Tarsus was a city—Acts 9:11; 11:25; 21:39)

16. Women at the tomb that first Easter were Mary, Salome, and Sarah. (Sarah was not; she was the wife of Abraham—Genesis 18:11; Mark 16:1)

17. Some of the sons of Jacob were Benjamin, Judah, and Esau. (Esau was his brother—Genesis 25:25-26)

18. The sons of King David included Absalom, Amnon, and Naaman. (Naaman was not; he was a Syrian captain—2 Kings 5:1; 2 Samuel 13:1)

19. Some of those at the cross of Jesus were Mary, John, and Peter. (Peter was not; he left—Matthew 26:75; John 19:25-27)

20. Disciples in the upper room when Jesus first appeared were Peter, Thomas, and James. (Thomas was not there until later—John 20:24, 26)

21. Kings to whom Paul preached the Gospel were Agrippa, Felix, and Herod. (Not to Herod—Acts 24:25-26; 25:13, 23)

4

22. Countries Paul visited on his missionary journeys included Italy, Greece, and Iran. (Iran was not mentioned—Acts 27: 1; 17:15)

23. Among early converts in the Christian Church were these women: Lydia, Priscilla, and Ruth. (Ruth lived in the days of the judges—Ruth 1:4)

24. Kings of Israel included Ahab, Athaliah, and Jeroboam. (Athaliah was a queen in Judah—2 Kings 11; 1 Kings 12: 20; 16:29)

25. Mountains in Palestine were Mount Sinai, Mount Hermon, and Mount Moriah. (Mount Sinai was outside Palestine— Exodus 19)

26. Some of the Ten Commandments are: not to steal; not to kill; not to take bribes. (Bribes are not included—Exodus 20:1-17)

27. The following persons were Samaritans: the woman at the well, one of the ten lepers who were healed, the man at the pool of Bethesda. (The man at the pool was not—John 5:2-9; 4:7-9; Luke 17:12-16)

28. Some familiar publicans were Simeon, Zacchaeus, and Matthew (Levi). (Simeon was not a publican—Luke 2: 25; 5:27; 19:2)

29. Parables of Jesus included a pearl, a net, and a sword. (The sword was not used as a parable—Matthew 10:34)

30. David was married to Michal, Bathsheba, and Deborah. (Not to Deborah; she was a judge—Judges 4-5)

31. The following disciples were fishermen: James, Matthew, and Andrew. (Matthew [Levi] was a tax collector—Luke 5:27; Mark 1:16, 19)

32. Queens mentioned in the Bible include Esther, Naomi, and Vashti. (Naomi was not a queen—Ruth 1; Esther 2:17)

33. The Israelites cast into the fiery furnace were Shadrach, Micah, and Abednego. (Micah was a minor prophet— Micah 1:1)

34. The brothers of Joseph included Reuben, Benjamin, and Jacob. (Jacob was his father—Genesis 35:21-26)
35. The sons of Naomi were Nahum, Mahlon, and Chilion. (Nahum was not; he was a prophet—Nahum 1:1; Ruth 1:2)
36. Plagues visited upon Egypt were frogs, lice, and ants. (Ants were not included—Exodus 7-12)
37. Jesus spoke in the villages of Capernaum, Cana, and Cyprus. (Cyprus is an island—Acts 13:4)
38. The first three sons of Adam were Cain, Enos, and Abel. (Seth was the third; Enos was a son of Seth—Genesis 4:25-26)
39. Mothers of the Bible include Eve, Hannah, and Lydia. (The Bible does not say if Lydia had children—Acts 16:14)
40. Animals mentioned in the Bible include the lion, the zebra, and the bear. (The zebra is not mentioned)
41. The wives of King Ahasuerus were Jezebel, Vashti, and Esther. (Jezebel was the wife of Ahab—1 Kings 16:30-31; Esther 2:17)
42. Grains spoken of in the Bible include corn, rice, and barley. (Rice is not mentioned)
43. Some of the major prophets of the Bible are Isaiah, Jeremiah, and Lamentations. (Lamentations is the name of a book written by Jeremiah)
44. Babylonian kings that Daniel served under were Nebuchadnezzar, Shalmaneser, and Belshazzar. (Shalmaneser was an Assyrian king—2 Kings 17:3; Daniel 1:1; 5:1-13)
45. Friends of Job were Eliphaz, Bildad, and Elijah. (Elijah lived later and was a prophet—1 Kings 17:1; Job 2:11)
46. The sons of Abraham were Issachar, Ishmael, and Isaac. (Issachar was a son of Jacob—Genesis 35:23; 16:15; 21:2-3)
47. The wise men brought gifts of myrrh, aloes, and gold. (Aloes was not one; frankincense was—Matthew 2:11)

48. Miriam's brothers included Moses, Aaron, and Hur. (Hur was not—Exodus 17:10-12; 6:20; 15:20)
49. Parts of the Christian's armor include the helmet, the buckler, and the shield. (The buckler is not included—Ephesians 6:10-17)
50. Some of the cities visited by Paul were Athens, Andronicus, and Corinth. (Andronicus was a person—Romans 16:7)

Who Said It?

The following quizzes are all familiar quotations from the Bible. The first set consists of quotations from famous Bible characters, taken from their spoken conversation. The second set is quotations from the words of Christ; the purpose is to identify the person to whom the words were spoken. The third set is familiar Bible phrases; the purpose is to see who can first give the name of the person who spoke them. The quizzes may be used in church groups, youth meetings, family groups, or between individuals. If some are too difficult, Bibles and concordances may be used to locate the quotations.

I. WHO SAID IT?

1. "Almost thou persuadest me to be a Christian." (King Agrippa—Acts 26:28)
2. "I will arise and go to my father." (Prodigal son—Luke 15:18)
3. "Lord, remember me when thou comest into thy kingdom." (Thief on the cross—Luke 23:42)
4. "Whither thou goest, I will go; and where thou lodgest, I will lodge." (Ruth—Ruth 1:16)
5. "Who knoweth whether thou art come to the kingdom for such a time as this?" (Mordecai—Esther 4:14)
6. "Except a man be born again, he cannot see the kingdom of God." (Jesus—John 3:3)
7. "Have thou nothing to do with that just man." (Pilate's wife—Matthew 27:19)
8. "Where art thou?" (God—Genesis 3:9)
9. "Yea, Lord; thou knowest that I love thee." (Peter—John 21:15)

10. "Who am I, that I should go unto Pharaoh?" (Moses—Exodus 3:11)
11. "Out of the eater came forth meat, and out of the strong came forth sweetness." (Samson—Judges 14:14)
12. "Where is he that is born King of the Jews?" (Wise men—Matthew 2:2)
13. "I am the voice of one crying in the wilderness." (John the Baptist—John 1:23)
14. "I will be like the most High." (Lucifer—Isaiah 14:14)
15. "Come over . . . and help us." (Man from Macedonia—Acts 16:9)
16. "This is my beloved Son, in whom I am well pleased." (God—Matthew 3:17)
17. "Thou shalt call his name JESUS: for he shall save his people from their sins." (Gabriel—Matthew 1:21)
18. "Is thy God, whom thou servest continually, able to deliver thee from the lions?" (Darius—Daniel 6:20)
19. "Behold the fire and the wood: but where is the lamb for a burnt offering?" (Isaac—Genesis 22:7)
20. "What is truth?" (Pilate—John 18:38)
21. "And if I perish, I perish." (Esther—Esther 4:16)
22. "Lord, lay not this sin to their charge." (Stephen—Acts 7:60)
23. "I shall go to him, but he shall not return to me." (David—2 Samuel 12:23)
24. "What I have written I have written." (Pilate—John 19:22)
25. "Am I my brother's keeper?" (Cain—Genesis 4:9)
26. "Behold, the half was not told me." (Queen of Sheba—1 Kings 10:7)
27. "Whatsoever he saith unto you, do it." (Mary—John 2:5)
28. "Speak; for thy servant heareth." (Samuel—1 Samuel 3:10)
29. "Wilt thou also destroy the righteous with the wicked?" (Abraham—Genesis 18:23)

30. "Oh that one would give me drink of the water of the well of Bethlehem." (David—2 Samuel 23:15)
31. "Understandest thou what thou readest?" (Philip—Acts 8:30)
32. "I have played the fool." (Saul—1 Samuel 26:21)
33. "I have seen God face to face." (Jacob—Genesis 32:30)
34. "Thou art weighed in the balances, and art found wanting." (Daniel—Daniel 5:27)
35. "Behold the Lamb of God, which taketh away the sin of the world." (John the Baptist—John 1:29)
36. "Shall I crucify your King?" (Pilate—John 19:15)
37. "Woman, I know him not." (Peter—Luke 22:57)
38. "What profit is it if we slay our brother, and conceal his blood?" (Judah—Genesis 37:26)
39. "What will ye give me, and I will deliver him unto you?" (Judas—Matthew 26:15)
40. "Curse God, and die." (Job's wife—Job 2:9)
41. "My punishment is greater than I can bear." (Cain—Genesis 4:13)
42. "Am I a dog, that thou comest to me with staves?" (Goliath—1 Samuel 17:43)
43. "Lord, what wilt thou have me to do?" (Paul—Acts 9:6)
44. "Who is on the Lord's side?" (Moses—Exodus 32:26)
45. "I go a fishing." (Peter—John 21:3)
46. "Did not we cast three men bound into the midst of the fire?" (Nebuchadnezzar—Daniel 3:24)
47. "I pray thee, let a double portion of thy spirit be upon me." (Elisha—2 Kings 2:9)
48. "Would God I had died for thee!" (David—2 Samuel 18:33)
49. "Silver and gold have I none; but such as I have give I thee." (Peter—Acts 3:6)
50. "What must I do to be saved?" (Philippian jailer—Acts 16:30)

II. TO WHOM DID JESUS SAY:

1. "Neither do I condemn thee: go, and sin no more." (To the woman taken in adultery—John 8:11)
2. "That thou doest, do quickly." (To Judas—John 13:27)
3. "Whosoever drinketh of the water that I shall give him shall never thirst." (To the woman at the well—John 4:14)
4. "Wist ye not that I must be about my Father's business?" (To Mary and Joseph—Luke 2:49)
5. "Suffer it to be so now: for thus it becometh us to fulfill all righteousness." (To John the Baptist—Matthew 3:15)
6. "Lovest thou me more than these?" (To Peter—John 21:15)
7. "Behold an Israelite indeed, in whom is no guile!" (To Nathanael—John 1:47)
8. "Woman, what have I to do with thee?" (To Mary—John 2:4)
9. "Marvel not that I said unto thee, Ye must be born again." (To Nicodemus—John 3:7)
10. "To day shalt thou be with me in paradise." (To the thief on the cross—Luke 23:43)
11. "O fools, and slow of heart to believe all that the prophets have spoken." (To disciples on Emmaus road—Luke 24:25)
12. "Make haste, and come down; for to day I must abide at thy house." (To Zacchaeus—Luke 19:5)
13. "Behold thy mother!" (To John—John 19:27)
14. "Woman, why weepest thou? Whom seekest thou?" (To Mary Magdalene—John 20:15)
15. "It is written again, Thou shalt not tempt the Lord thy God." (To the devil—Matthew 4:7)

16. "O thou of little faith, wherefore didst thou doubt?" (To Peter—Matthew 14:31)

17. "Thou couldest have no power at all against me, except it were given thee from above." (To Pilate—John 19:11)

18. "Betrayest thou the Son of man with a kiss?" (To Judas—Luke 22:48)

19. "Have I been so long time with you, and yet hast thou not known me?" (To Philip—John 14:9)

20. "What is that to thee? Follow thou me." (To Peter—John 21:22)

21. "Reach hither thy finger, and behold my hands." (To Thomas—John 20:27)

22. "Go and sell that thou hast, and give to the poor . . . and come and follow me." (To the rich young ruler—Matthew 19:21)

23. "If these should hold their peace, the stones would immediately cry out." (To some Pharisees—Luke 19:40)

24. "Will ye also go away?" (To the disciples—John 6:67)

25. "Whence shall we buy bread, that these may eat?" (To Philip—John 6:5)

26. "Arise, take up thy bed, and go unto thine house." (To the man with the palsy—Matthew 9:6)

27. "I am the resurrection, and the life." (To Martha—John 11:25)

28. "If I wash thee not, thou hast no part with me." (To Peter—John 13:8)

29. "Why hast thou forsaken me?" (To God—Matthew 27:46)

30. "Behold, Satan hath desired to have you, that he may sift you as wheat." (To Peter—Luke 22:31)

III. WHO SPOKE THESE WORDS?

1. "I know that my redeemer liveth." (Job—Job 19:25)
2. "Train up a child in the way he should go." (Solomon—Proverbs 22:6)
3. "His name shall be called Wonderful." (Isaiah—Isaiah 9:6)
4. "The eternal God is thy refuge, and underneath are the everlasting arms." (Moses—Deuteronomy 33:27)
5. "The LORD is my shepherd; I shall not want." (David—Psalm 23:1)
6. "Come unto me, all ye that labour and are heavy laden, and I will give you rest." (Jesus—Matthew 11:28)
7. "The wages of sin is death; but the gift of God is eternal life." (Paul—Romans 6:23)
8. "Can two walk together, except they be agreed?" (The Lord—Amos 3:3)
9. "Thou art weighed in the balances, and art found wanting." (Daniel—Daniel 5:27)
10. "Thy words were found, and I did eat them." (Jeremiah—Jeremiah 15:16)
11. "This book of the law shall not depart out of thy mouth." (God—Joshua 1:8)
12. "The LORD watch between me and thee, when we are absent one from another." (Laban—Genesis 31:49)
13. "Be ye doers of the word, and not hearers only." (James—James 1:22)
14. "Woe is me! For I am undone; because I am a man of unclean lips." (Isaiah—Isaiah 6:5)
15. "When I see the blood, I will pass over you." (The Lord—Exodus 12:13)

13

16. "It is the blood that maketh an atonement for the soul." (The Lord—Leviticus 17:11)
17. "His mouth is most sweet: yea, he is altogether lovely." (The Shulamite girl—Song of Solomon 5:16)
18. "Ho, every one that thirsteth, come ye to the waters." (The Lord—Isaiah 55:1)
19. "Is it nothing to you, all ye that pass by?" (Jeremiah—Lamentations 1:12)
20. "Trust in the Lord with all thine heart; and lean not unto thine own understanding." (Solomon—Proverbs 3:5)
21. "And let the beauty of the Lord our God be upon us." (Moses—Psalm 90:17)
22. "Prepare to meet thy God." (The Lord—Amos 4:12)
23. "Neither is there salvation in any other: for there is none other name under heaven given among men, whereby we must be saved." (Peter—Acts 4:12)
24. "We love him, because he first loved us." (John—1 John 4:19)
25. "God forbid that I should glory, save in the cross of our Lord Jesus Christ." (Paul—Galatians 6:14)
26. "The Lord is good, a strong hold in the day of trouble." (Nahum—Nahum 1:7)
27. "The Lord is in his holy temple: let all the earth keep silence before him." (The Lord—Habakkuk 2:20)
28. "Not by might, nor by power, but by my spirit, saith the Lord of hosts." (Angel—Zechariah 4:6)
29. "He is despised and rejected of men; a man of sorrows, and acquainted with grief." (Isaiah—Isaiah 53:3)
30. "If a man die, shall he live again?" (Job—Job 14:14)

Take a Number

This is a quiz program on numbers mentioned in the Bible. The contestant or team is asked to choose a number from one to ten. The questions all have to do with the number chosen. The contestant or team should attempt to answer all seven questions given it. The questions may be placed in boxes or envelopes numbered from one to ten, and selected from the box of the chosen number. An award may be given to the person or team getting all questions correct from the chosen number. Now, get someone to "Take a Number"—any number from one to ten!

NUMBER ONE

1. Nathan told David of a poor man who had one little what? (Ewe lamb—2 Samuel 12:3)
2. Jesus said not one jot or one tittle of what shall ever fail? (The Law—Matthew 5:18)
3. God is not willing that one of these little ones should what? (Perish—Matthew 18:14)
4. The prodigal son asked to be made as one of what? (Hired servants—Luke 15:19)
5. Jesus said there shall be one fold and one what? (Shepherd—John 10:16)
6. There is one God and one Mediator between God and what? (Men—1 Timothy 2:5)
7. Which one of the disciples smote the servant of the high priest? (Peter—Luke 22:50)

NUMBER TWO

1. What woman hid two Israelite spies in Jericho? (Rahab—Joshua 2:1-4)
2. Jesus said that no man can serve two what? (Masters—Matthew 6:24)
3. To what village were the two disciples going when Jesus met them? (Emmaus—Luke 24:13)
4. Into what city did the two angels go to seek Lot? (Sodom—Genesis 19:1)
5. Ephraim and Manasseh were the two sons of whom? (Joseph—Genesis 41:50-52)
6. Who tore the two pillars of a temple down to slay the Philistines? (Samson—Judges 16:29)
7. Elkanah had two wives, one named Peninnah, the other what? (Hannah—1 Samuel 1:2)

NUMBER THREE

1. Who smote his ass three times and it spoke out? (Balaam—Numbers 22:28)
2. What were the names of Noah's three sons? (Shem, Ham, Japheth—Genesis 6:10)
3. When Moses stretched forth his hand there was darkness three days in what land? (Egypt—Exodus 10:22)
4. Three of David's mighty men brought water from what well? (Bethlehem—2 Samuel 23:16)
5. Eliphaz, Bildad, and Zophar were the three friends of whom? (Job—Job 2:11)
6. What prophet stretched himself three times upon a child to restore his life? (Elijah—1 Kings 17:18-21)
7. Who wanted to make three tabernacles on the mount of transfiguration? (Peter—Matthew 17:4)

NUMBER FOUR

1. What man, who had been dead four days, was raised by Jesus? (Lazarus—John 11:14-17)
2. From what besieged city did the four lepers flee in order to find plenty? (Samaria—2 Kings 7:1-3)
3. Who was the fourth person Nebuchadnezzar saw in the fiery furnace? (Son of God—Daniel 3:25)
4. Who saw a sheet full of animals let down from heaven by its four corners? (Peter—Acts 10:11)
5. Who was the prisoner on the ship which cast out its four anchors? (Paul—Acts 27:29)
6. Who promised to restore his ill-gotten means fourfold? (Zacchaeus—Luke 19:8)
7. Jesus said, Say not ye "There are four months" until what? (Harvest—John 4:35)

NUMBER FIVE

1. Who chose five smooth stones to slay a great giant? (David—1 Samuel 17:40)
2. What great king wrote a thousand and five songs? (Solomon—1 Kings 4:32)
3. Who was taken captive by five kings and rescued by Abraham? (Lot—Genesis 14:8-16)
4. One man made an excuse, saying that he had bought five yoke of what? (Oxen—Luke 14:19)
5. What pool with five porches had waters famed for healing? (Bethesda—John 5:2)
6. What apostle received thirty-nine stripes on five different occasions? (Paul—2 Corinthians 11:24)
7. What woman was told by Jesus that she had had five husbands? (Woman at the well—John 4:18)

NUMBER SIX

1. At what wedding were there six waterpots of stone? (Cana of Galilee—John 2:1-6)
2. What giant was six cubits and a span in height? (Goliath—1 Samuel 17:4)
3. To whom did the angel Gabriel appear in the sixth month? (Mary—Luke 1:26-27)
4. What was Israel to gather on six days, but not on the seventh? (Manna—Exodus 16:26)
5. What three disciples did Jesus take into the mount after six days? (Peter, James, John—Matthew 17:1)
6. Who was praying on a rooftop in Joppa at about the sixth hour? (Peter—Acts 10:9)
7. Each of the four beasts about the throne of God had six what? (Wings—Revelation 4:8)

NUMBER SEVEN

1. What Syrian captain washed in the Jordan River seven times to be cured of leprosy? (Naaman—2 Kings 5:9-14)
2. Who was seen in the midst of the seven golden candlesticks? (Christ—Revelation 1:13)
3. Out of whom had Jesus cast seven devils? (Mary Magdalene—Mark 16:9)
4. In whose dream were seen seven ears of corn on one stalk? (Pharaoh's—Genesis 41:5)
5. What city did Israel encompass seven times on the seventh day? (Jericho—Joshua 6:4)
6. How many were fed with the seven loaves and a few fishes? (4,000—Matthew 15:36)
7. For whom did Jacob offer to serve Laban seven years? (Rachel—Genesis 29:18)

NUMBER EIGHT

1. What boy king began to reign when he was eight years old? (Josiah—2 Kings 22:1)
2. What disciple doubted Jesus was alive until he saw him eight days later? (Thomas—John 20:26)
3. Who raised Aeneas after he had been sick of palsy eight years? (Peter—Acts 9:32-34)
4. Which son of Abraham was circumcised when eight days old? (Isaac—Genesis 21:4)
5. In whose mammoth ship were only eight persons saved? (Noah's—1 Peter 3:20)
6. What child was circumcised and received his name when eight days old? (Jesus—Luke 2:21)
7. Who was David's father, who had eight sons? (Jesse—1 Samuel 17:12)

NUMBER NINE

1. Of the ten lepers cleansed, nine failed to return to do what? (Give thanks—Luke 17:17)
2. Who lived to be 969 years old? (Methuselah—Genesis 5:27)
3. What king slept in an iron bedstead nine cubits long? (Og—Deuteronomy 3:11)
4. What ancient Assyrian city begins with the word nine? (Nineveh—Jonah 1:2)
5. What land west of the Jordan was given to nine and a half tribes? (Canaan—Numbers 34:1-2, 12-13)
6. What kingdom fell captive to Assyria after Hoshea's nine-year reign? (Israel—2 Kings 17:6)
7. What city did Israel rebuild after the captivity, but nine parts of the people lived without it? (Jerusalem—Nehemiah 11:1)

NUMBER TEN

1. What city would God have spared had He found ten righteous persons therein? (Sodom—Genesis 18:20-23, 32)
2. Who asked to see the sun's shadow go backward ten degrees? (Hezekiah—2 Kings 20:10)
3. Who proved his chosen diet was better in ten days? (Daniel—Daniel 1:12)
4. What widow and her family dwelt ten years in Moab? (Naomi—Ruth 1:4)
5. Of the ten pieces of silver the woman had, how many were lost? (One—Luke 15:8)
6. Whose ten brothers came down to Egypt to buy grain? (Joseph's—Genesis 42:3-4)
7. Who asked his wife if he were not better than ten sons? (Elkanah—1 Samuel 1:8)

Is It in the Bible?

This quiz is a knowledge test of what is and what is not in the Bible. It may be used in large or small groups, in Sunday school classes or assemblies, in youth groups or class meetings. It may be oral with hands raised, or it may be duplicated with copies given out and answers given at a later time. It may be surprising to the participants to learn of all the things that are in the Bible and to find that some things they thought were in the Bible, are not! Make it enjoyable, not a test of the participants' Bible knowledge, though they will learn much from it. Many spiritual applications may be made from the different things in the Bible and the way they were used.

Note: Many of these names used in the King James Bible do not refer to the actual plant, animal, or object that we are familiar with today. For example, "lily of the valleys" does not mean the well-known white-belled spring flower but is an undetermined garden flower; "elm" refers to a semidesert tree, the terebinth; and "girdle" is a type of wrap-around belt, not an undergarment. Questions in regard to such terms can be answered by consulting a Bible dictionary.

I. ANIMALS

1. Cat? (No)
2. Dog? (Yes—Luke 16:21; 2 Peter 2:22)
3. Bear? (Yes—1 Samuel 17:36; 2 Kings 2:24)
4. Horse? (Yes—Exodus 14:23; James 3:3)
5. Goat? (Yes—Genesis 27:9; Matthew 25:33)
6. Monkey? (No)
7. Zebra? (No)
8. Hare? (Yes—Leviticus 11:6; Deuteronomy 14:7)
9. Elephant? (No)
10. Camel? (Yes—Genesis 24:10; Matthew 19:24)
11. Fox? (Yes—Judges 15:4; Matthew 8:20)
12. Lion? (Yes—Genesis 49:9; 1 Peter 5:8)
13. Leopard? (Yes—Isaiah 11:6; Revelation 13:2)
14. Sheep? (Yes—Genesis 30:32; John 10)
15. Pig? (No; but swine, yes—Matthew 7:6; 8:30)

II. FOODS

1. Rice? (No)
2. Potatoes? (No)
3. Bread? (Yes—Matthew 4:4; 26:26)
4. Butter? (Yes—Genesis 18:8; Proverbs 30:33)
5. Cheese? (Yes—1 Samuel 17:18; Job 10:10)
6. Honey? (Yes—Exodus 3:8; Judges 14:18)
7. Milk? (Yes—Numbers 13:27; 1 Peter 2:2)
8. Bananas? (No)
9. Onions? (Yes—Numbers 11:5)
10. Cinnamon? (Yes—Exodus 30:23; Proverbs 7:17)
11. Grapes? (Yes—Song of Solomon 2:13; Genesis 40:11)
12. Olives? (Yes—James 3:12; Romans 11:24)
13. Apples? (Yes—Proverbs 25:11; Song of Solomon 2:5)
14. Barley? (Yes—Ruth 1:22; John 6:9)
15. Lettuce? (No)

III. BIRDS

1. Swan? (Yes—Leviticus 11:18; Deuteronomy 14:16)
2. Peacock? (Yes—1 Kings 10:22; Job 39:13)
3. Dove? (Yes—Psalm 68:13; Song of Solomon 6:9)
4. Pigeon? (Yes—Genesis 15:9; Luke 2:24)
5. Sparrow? (Yes—Psalm 84:3; Matthew 10:29)
6. Wren? (No)
7. Raven? (Yes—Genesis 8:7; 1 Kings 17:4)
8. Stork? (Yes—Leviticus 11:19; Psalm 104:17)
9. Eagle? (Yes—Isaiah 40:31; Proverbs 23:5)
10. Hawk? (Yes—Leviticus 11:16; Job 39:26)
11. Ostrich? (Yes—Job 39:13; Lamentations 4:3)
12. Owl? (Yes—Leviticus 11:16; Isaiah 13:21)
13. Parrot? (No)
14. Pelican? (Yes—Leviticus 11:18; Deuteronomy 14:17)
15. Duck? (No)

IV. PLANTS

1. Rose? (Yes—Song of Solomon 2:1)
2. Tulip? (No)
3. Daisy? (No)
4. Lily? (Yes—Matthew 6:28-29; Song of Solomon 5:13)
5. Violet? (No)
6. Mustard? (Yes—Matthew 13:31)
7. Daffodil? (No)
8. Thistles? (Yes—Genesis 3:17-18)
9. Lily of valley? (Yes—Song of Solomon 2:1-2)
10. Iris? (No)
11. Camphire? (Yes—Song of Solomon 1:14)
12. Flax? (Yes—Exodus 9:31; Joshua 2:6)
13. Crocus? (No; possibly "saffron" in Song of Solomon 4:14 refers to it)
14. Spikenard? (Yes—John 12:3)
15. Aloes? (Yes—John 19:39; Psalm 45:8)

V. INSECTS

1. Ants? (Yes—Proverbs 6:6; 30:25)
2. Locusts? (Yes—Matthew 3:4; Exodus 10:4)
3. Caterpillars? (Yes—Joel 1:4; Psalm 105:34)
4. Flea? (Yes—1 Samuel 24:14; 26:20)
5. Flies? (Yes—Exodus 8:21; Psalm 78:45)
6. Lice? (Yes—Exodus 8:16; Psalm 105:31)
7. Bees? (Yes—Judges 14:8; Psalm 118:12)
8. Beetles? (Yes—Leviticus 11:22)
9. Grasshopper? (Yes—Leviticus 11:22; Numbers 13:33)
10. Butterfly? (No)
11. Spider? (Yes—Proverbs 30:28; Job 8:14)
12. Hornet? (Yes—Exodus 23:28; Joshua 24:12)
13. Moth? (Yes—Matthew 6:19; Psalm 39:11)
14. Wasp? (No)
15. Scorpion? (Yes—Luke 11:12; Revelation 9:10)

VI. TOOLS

1. Plow? (Yes—Luke 9:62; Deuteronomy 22:10)
2. Rake? (No)
3. Ladder? (Yes—Genesis 28:12)
4. Hoe? (No)
5. Saw? (Yes—2 Samuel 12:31)
6. Nail? (Yes—Judges 4:21; John 20:25)
7. Hammer? (Yes—Judges 4:21; 1 Kings 6:7)
8. Axe? (Yes—1 Kings 6:7; 2 Kings 6:5)
9. Anvil? (Yes—Isaiah 41:7)
10. Scissors? (No)
11. Sickle? (Yes—Deuteronomy 16:9; Mark 4:29)
12. Scythe? (No)
13. Awl? (Yes—Exodus 21:6; Deuteronomy 15:17)
14. Knives? (Yes—Joshua 5:2; Genesis 22:10)
15. Screwdriver? (No)

VII. SAYINGS

1. The skin of my teeth. (Yes—Job 19:20)
2. One among a thousand. (Yes—Job 33:23)
3. The apple of his eye. (Yes—Deuteronomy 32:10)
4. Make it good. (Yes—Numbers 23:19)
5. What aileth thee? (Yes—2 Kings 6:28)
6. Fled for their life? (Yes—2 Kings 7:7)
7. Beat to pieces. (Yes—Isaiah 3:15)
8. Woe is me! (Yes—Isaiah 6:5)
9. A drop of a bucket. (Yes—Isaiah 40:15)
10. Two are better than one. (Yes—Ecclesiastes 4:9)
11. Lick the dust. (Yes—Micah 7:17)
12. Good for nothing. (Yes—Matthew 5:13)
13. Wrap it up. (Yes—Micah 7:3)
14. Half dead. (Yes—Luke 10:30)
15. See eye to eye. (Yes—Isaiah 52:8)

VIII. TREES

1. Oak? (Yes—Genesis 35:4; 2 Samuel 18:9)
2. Sycamore? (Yes—Luke 19:4; Psalm 78:47)
3. Olive? (Yes—Judges 9:9; Psalm 52:8)
4. Palm? (Yes—Exodus 15:27; Deuteronomy 34:3)
5. Mulberry? (Yes—2 Samuel 5:23)
6. Fig? (Yes—Judges 9:10; 1 Kings 4:25)
7. Almond? (Yes—Numbers 17:8; Ecclesiastes 12:5)
8. Elm? (Yes—Hosea 4:13)
9. Cedar? (Yes—1 Kings 4:33; Isaiah 2:13)
10. Fir? (Yes—Isaiah 14:8; Hosea 14:8)
11. Locust? (No)
12. Willow? (Yes—Leviticus 23:40; Psalm 137:2)
13. Pine? (Yes—Isaiah 41:19; Isaiah 60:13)
14. Chestnut? (Yes—Genesis 30:37; Ezekiel 31:8)
15. Myrtle? (Yes—Nehemiah 8:15; Isaiah 41:19)

IX. PARTS OF THE BODY

1. Nose? (Yes—Psalm 115:6; Proverbs 30:33)
2. Ear? (Yes—Psalm 115:6; Matthew 28:14)
3. Arm? (Yes—Luke 1:51; John 12:38)
4. Eyes? (Yes—2 Chronicles 16:9; John 9:10)
5. Lips? (Yes—Psalm 141:3; Matthew 15:8)
6. Tongue? (Yes—Psalm 137:6; Philippians 2:11)
7. Toe? (Yes—Daniel 2:41; Judges 1:6)
8. Fingers? (Yes—Isaiah 2:8; John 20:25)
9. Feet? (Yes—Genesis 49:10; Matthew 10:14)
10. Elbow? (No)
11. Heart? (Yes—Psalm 19:14; Matthew 5:8)
12. Knees? (Yes—Daniel 5:6; Luke 5:8)
13. Cheek? (Yes—Job 16:10; Matthew 5:39)
14. Hair? (Yes—Daniel 3:27; Matthew 5:36)
15. Ankle? (Yes—Ezekiel 47:3; Acts 3:7)

X. CLOTHING

1. Girdle (a type of belt)? (Yes—2 Kings 1:8; Matthew 3:4)
2. Shoes? (Yes—Exodus 3:5; Matthew 3:11)
3. Hat? (Yes—Daniel 3:21)
4. Gloves? (No)
5. Belt? (No)
6. Pants? (No)
7. Socks? (No—"hosen" in Daniel 3:21 refers to trousers)
8. Coat? (Yes—Genesis 3:21; Matthew 5:40)
9. Skirt? (Yes—1 Samuel 15:27; Zechariah 8:23)
10. Scarf? (No)
11. Boots? (No—"booties" in Habakkuk 2:7 refers to plunder)
12. Shirt? (No)
13. Robe? (Yes—Luke 15:22; Matthew 27:28)
14. Bonnet? (Yes—Exodus 29:9; Ezekiel 44:18)
15. Garter? (No)

XI. PROVERBS

1. Let your conscience be your guide. (No)
2. God helps those that help themselves (No)
3. Godliness with contentment is great gain. (Yes—1 Timothy 6:6)
4. Practice what you preach. (No)
5. Do unto others as you would have them do unto you. (No—but see Matthew 7:12)
6. Where there's a will there's a way. (No)
7. All things come to him who waits. (No)
8. Cleanliness is next to godliness. (No)
9. A good name is rather to be chosen than great riches. (Yes—Proverbs 22:1)
10. Do all things without murmurings and disputings. (Yes—Philippians 2:14)
11. The better the day the better the deed. (No)
12. A word to the wise is sufficient. (No)
13. Where your treasure is, there will your heart be also. (Yes—Matthew 6:21)
14. In God we trust. (No)
15. Be moderate in all things. (No—but see Philippians 4:5)

XII. MINERALS

1. Diamonds? (Yes—Exodus 28:18; Jeremiah 17:1)
2. Onyx? (Yes—Genesis 2:12; Job 28:16)
3. Ruby? (Yes—Job 28:18; Proverbs 3:15)
4. Gold? (Yes—Acts 3:6; 1 Peter 1:18)
5. Silver? (Yes—Acts 3:6; 1 Peter 1:18)
6. Platinum? (No)
7. Sapphire? (Yes—Exodus 24:10; Revelation 21:19)
8. Emerald? (Yes—Exodus 28:18; Revelation 21:19)
9. Jasper? (Yes—Exodus 28:20)
10. Aluminum? (No)
11. Copper? (Yes—Ezra 8:27; 2 Timothy 4:14)
12. Topaz? (Yes—Exodus 28:17; Revelation 21:20)
13. Iron? (Yes—Genesis 4:22; Acts 12:10)
14. Amethyst? (Yes—Exodus 28:19; Revelation 21:20)
15. Pearl? (Yes—Matthew 7:6; 13:46)

Search for Me

Try a different approach with this new quiz called "Search for Me." It may be used with adults or young people, and even with children in some instances. Each person must have his own Bible. The idea is to be able to locate different things in the Bible. Most of the things to be located are familiar, but some may require the use of a concordance. The object to be located is announced to the group, and the first person to find it in the Bible must give the location (the chapter and verse as well as the book of the Bible). Insist that each object be found in the Bible before the location is announced. The group may be divided into sides, and a score be kept during the quiz. There are ten quizzes included on familiar persons, places, and things in the Bible, and they may be used over a period of ten weeks or as often as the group meets. Try them in family worship to create interest in the Bible and to increase familiarity with its contents.

I. FAMILIAR PLACES IN THE BIBLE

(Find these familiar places mentioned in the Bible)

1. Cana of Galilee (John 2)
2. Garden of Eden (Genesis 2)
3. Red Sea (Exodus 14)
4. Gaza (Acts 8)
5. Emmaus (Luke 24)
6. Sodom (Genesis 19)
7. Jericho (Joshua 2)
8. Mount Nebo (Deuteronomy 34)
9. Uz (Job 1)
10. Nineveh (Jonah 1)

II. FAMILIAR MESSIANIC TITLES

(Find these familiar titles of Christ in the Old Testament)

1. Rose of Sharon (Song of Solomon 2:1)
2. Prince of Peace (Isaiah 9:6)
3. Shiloh (Genesis 49:10)
4. Immanuel (Isaiah 7:14)
5. Star of Jacob (Numbers 24:17)
6. Messiah (Daniel 9:25)
7. Redeemer (Job 19:25)
8. Son of God (Daniel 3:25)
9. Man of sorrows (Isaiah 53:3)
10. Son of righteousness (Malachi 4:2)

III. FAMILIAR PARABLES OF JESUS

(Find these familiar parables in the gospels)

1. The prodigal son (Luke 15)
2. The Good Shepherd (John 10)
3. The ten virgins (Matthew 25)
4. The good Samaritan (Luke 10)
5. The sower (Matthew 13; Mark 4; Luke 8)
6. The house on the rock (Matthew 7)
7. The rich man and Lazarus (Luke 16)
8. The talents (Matthew 25)
9. The pearl of great price (Matthew 13)
10. The lost sheep (Matthew 18; Luke 15)

IV. FAMILIAR CHAPTERS OF THE BIBLE

(Find these familiar chapters in God's Word)

1. Love chapter (1 Corinthians 13)
2. Faith chapter (Hebrews 11)
3. Suffering Servant (Isaiah 53)
4. Shepherd psalm (Psalm 23)
5. Resurrection chapter (1 Corinthians 15)
6. Forgiveness chapter (Psalm 51)
7. The Good Shepherd chapter (John 10)
8. The traveler's psalm (Psalm 121)
9. The heaven chapter (Revelation 21)
10. The creation chapter (Genesis 1)

V. FAMILIAR FRIENDS OF THE BIBLE

(Find these familiar persons in the Bible)

1. Zacchaeus (Luke 19)
2. Cornelius (Acts 10)
3. Melchizedek (Genesis 14)
4. Ethiopian eunuch (Acts 8)
5. Samson (Judges 13-14)
6. Simeon (Luke 2)
7. Gideon (Judges 6-8)
8. Baalam (Numbers 22)
9. Mordecai (Esther 2)
10. Shadrach (Daniel 3)

VI. FAMILIAR PASSAGES OF THE BIBLE

(Find these well-known portions of the Bible)

1. The Ten Commandments (Exodus 20)
2. The Beatitudes (Matthew 5)
3. Letters to the seven churches (Revelation 2-3)
4. Pentecost (Acts 2)
5. Olivet discourse (Matthew 24-25)
6. The virtuous woman (Proverbs 31)
7. The Sermon on the Mount (Matthew 5-7)
8. The Great Commission (Matthew 28:18-20)
9. The upper room discourse (John 14-16)
10. The Word of God (Psalm 119—a poem on the Word of God)

VII. FAMILIAR PROMISES OF THE BIBLE

(Find these familiar Bible verses in your Bible)

1. "And I give unto them eternal life; and they shall never perish, neither shall any man pluck them out of my hand." (John 10:28)
2. "Thou wilt keep him in perfect peace, whose mind is stayed on thee: because he trusteth in thee." (Isaiah 26:3)
3. "If we confess our sins, he is faithful and just to forgive us our sins, and to cleanse us from all unrighteousness." (1 John 1:9)
4. "Call unto me, and I will answer thee, and shew thee great and mighty things, which thou knowest not." (Jeremiah 33:3)
5. "The eternal God is thy refuge, and underneath are the everlasting arms." (Deuteronomy 33:27)
6. "And ye now therefore have sorrow: but I will see you again, and your heart shall rejoice, and your joy no man taketh from you." (John 16:22)
7. "I will instruct thee and teach thee in the way which thou shalt go: I will guide thee with mine eye." (Psalm 32:8)
8. "Come now, and let us reason together, saith the LORD: though your sins be as scarlet they shall be as white as snow; though they be red like crimson, they shall be as wool." (Isaiah 1:18)
9. "Trust in the LORD with all thine heart; and lean not unto thine own understanding. In all thy ways acknowledge him, and he shall direct thy paths." (Proverbs 3:5-6)
10. "Come unto me, all ye that labour and are heavy laden, and I will give you rest." (Matthew 11:28)

VIII. FAMILIAR MIRACLES OF CHRIST

(Find these miracles Christ performed in your Bible)

1. Feeding of the 5,000 (Matthew 14; Mark 6; Luke 9)
2. Walking on the sea (Matthew 14; Mark 6; John 6)
3. Blind man healed (John 9)
4. Water changed to wine (John 2)
5. Raising Lazarus from the dead (John 11)
6. Healing of the ten lepers (Luke 17:12)
7. Stilling of the sea (Matthew 8; Mark 4; Luke 8)
8. Miraculous drought of fishes (Luke 5)
9. Demoniac of Gadarenes healed (Matthew 8; Mark 5; Luke 8)
10. Healing of the palsied man (Matthew 9; Mark 2; Luke 5)

IX. FAMILIAR PRAYERS OF THE BIBLE

(Find where these prayers are located in the Bible)

1. The Lord's Prayer (Matthew 6)
2. Abraham's prayer for Sodom (Genesis 18)
3. David's prayer for forgiveness (Psalm 51)
4. Paul's prayer for healing (2 Corinthians 12)
5. Solomon's prayer for wisdom (1 Kings 3)
6. Simeon's prayer of thanksgiving (Luke 2)
7. Hannah's prayer for a son (1 Samuel 1)
8. Moses' prayer for deliverance from serpents (Numbers 21)
9. Our Lord's prayer in Gethsemane (Matthew 26:39)
10. Our Lord's prayer for His own (John 17)

X. FAMILIAR EVENTS OF THE BIBLE

(Find where these familiar events are recounted in the Bible)

1. The crossing of the Red Sea (Exodus 14)
2. Daniel in the Lion's den (Daniel 6)
3. Jonah in the great fish (Jonah 1)
4. Esther made queen of Persia (Esther 2)
5. Ruth gleans in the field (Ruth 2)
6. The fall of Jericho (Joshua 6)
7. The affliction of Job (Job 1)
8. The offering of Isaac (Genesis 22)
9. Noah's ark and the Flood (Genesis 6)
10. The fall of Samson (Judges 16)

It Figures

Figures can be fun as well as informative with these quizzes on Bible numbers. Copies must be duplicated for each person, and sufficient time given to find the answers in the Bible. Few of the numbers will be known from memory, but they can be located in the Bible from the clues given. The answer must then be worked out from the numbers located in the Bible. The correct answers, as well as the numbers and Bible references, are given at the end of this chapter. The quiz may be used over a period of twelve weeks, with a new quiz given out each week and the answers given at the Sunday evening service or on the following week.

I. FROM PHILISTINES TO THE FURNACE

1. Take the number of Philistines that Samson slew with the jawbone of an ass _____

2. Add the number of songs that the Bible says Solomon composed _____ = _____

3. Divide by the number of wise virgins who took oil in their lamps _____ = _____

4. Subtract Enoch's age before he was translated to heaven _____ = _____

5. Multiply by the number of times hotter the fiery furnace was heated _____ = _____

   AND THE ANSWER IS _____.

II. FROM DAYS TO PIECES OF SILVER

1. Take the number of days that Nineveh was given to repent at the preaching of Jonah _____

2. Add Josiah's age when he began to reign as king in Judah _____ = _____

3. Divide by the number of cities of refuge set aside in the land of Canaan _____ = _____

4. Subtract the number of men Joshua sent to spy out the city of Jericho _____ = _____

5. Add the number of pieces of silver Joseph was sold for by his brothers _____ = _____

   AND THE ANSWER IS _____.

III. FROM DAYS TO CUBITS

1. Take the number of days the Israelites wept for Moses when he died _____

2. Add the number of fish Peter drew into his net at Jesus' command _____ = _____

3. Divide by the times Elijah lay upon the child to restore his life _____ = _____

4. Subtract the number of green withs that were used to bind Samson _____ = _____

5. Divide by the number of cubits of Goliath's height. _____ = _____

   AND THE ANSWER IS _____.

IV. FROM HORSEMEN TO DAYS

1. Take the number of horsemen sent to guard Paul against the Jews _____
2. Multiply by the number of lepers who lay at the gate of Samaria in siege _____ = _____
3. Subtract the height in cubits of Noah's ark _____ = _____
4. Divide by the smallest number of righteous people Abraham pleaded for in Sodom _____ = _____
5. Multiply by the number of days that Job's friends tarried in silence _____ = _____

    AND THE ANSWER IS _____.

V. FROM YEARS TO BRANCHES

1. Take the number of years of Judah's captivity in Babylon _____
2. Multiply by the years Jacob served Laban for his cattle _____ = _____
3. Add the number of generations from Abraham to David, as given by Matthew _____ = _____
4. Divide by the times Elisha told Naaman to wash in the Jordan River _____ = _____
5. Multiply by the number of branches on the vine in the butler's dream _____ = _____

    AND THE ANSWER IS _____.

VI. FROM STONES TO YEARS

1. Take the number of stones taken from the Jordan River as a memorial _____

2. Multiply this by the degrees the shadow on the sundial went backward for Hezekiah _____ = _____

3. Add the number of men in the boat when Paul was shipwrecked _____ = _____

4. Divide by the number of steps on Solomon's throne _____ = _____

5. Subtract the years Jacob spent in the land of Egypt _____ = _____

AND THE ANSWER IS _____.

VII. FROM ARROWS TO JERICHO

1. Take the number of arrows Jonathan shot toward David _____

2. Multiply by the number of pots of water Jesus turned into wine _____ = _____

3. Divide by the number of men it took to carry the cluster of grapes in Canaan _____ = _____

4. Add the number of days Lazarus lay dead in the grave _____ = _____

5. Subtract the number of times Israel compassed Jericho on the seventh day _____ = _____

AND THE ANSWER IS _____.

VIII. FROM THE BEAST TO JACOB

1. Take the number that shall signify the mark of the beast

   _____

2. Divide it by the number of chains that bound Peter in prison _____ = _____

3. Subtract the length in cubits of King Og's iron bedstead

   _____ = _____

4. Add the number of lords entertained at Belshazzar's feast

   _____ = _____

5. Subtract the number of sons Jacob had _____ = _____

   AND THE ANSWER IS _____.

IX. FROM MEN TO YEARS

1. Take the number of men sent to take Jeremiah out of the dungeon _____

2. Add Joseph's age at the time of his death _____ =

   _____

3. Subtract the height of Haman's gallow prepared for Mordecai _____ = _____

4. Divide by the number of measures of barley Boaz gave to Ruth _____ = _____

5. Add the number of years Tyre should be forgotten _____

   = _____

   AND THE ANSWER IS _____.

X. FROM PROPHETS TO SONS

1. Take the number of prophets of Baal whom Elijah slew

   _____

2. Divide by the number of barley loaves the lad gave to
   Jesus _____ = _____

3. Add the number of men who remained in Gideon's band

   _____ = _____

4. Subtract the age which the Jews said Jesus had not yet
   reached _____ = _____

5. Divide by the number of the sons of Haman _____ =

   _____

AND THE ANSWER IS _____.

XI. FROM STARS TO DAYS

1. Take the number of stars that made obeisance to Joseph

   _____

2. Multiply by the number of porches at the pool of Bethesda

   _____ = _____

3. Add the number of years added to Hezekiah's life _____

   = _____

4. Divide by the number of stones David selected from the
   brook _____ = _____

5. Subtract the number of days Paul was without sight in
   Damascus _____ = _____

AND THE ANSWER IS _____.

XII. FROM DAYS TO DAUGHTERS

1. Take the number of days Rahab told the spies to hide in the mountain _____

2. Multiply the total number of barrels of water poured on the altar by Elijah _____ = _____

3. Subtract the number of days that Paul abode with Peter in Jerusalem _____ = _____

4. Add the furlongs between Bethany and Jerusalem _____ = _____

5. Divide by the number of Laban's daughters _____ = _____

AND THE ANSWER IS _____.

ANSWERS

I. 252

1. Take the number of Philistines (1,000—Judges 15:16)	1,000
2. Add the number of songs (1,005—1 Kings 4:32)	2,005
3. Divide by the wise virgins (5—Matthew 25:2)	401
4. Subtract Enoch's age (365—Genesis 5:23)	36
5. Multiply the times hotter (7—Daniel 3:19)	252

II. 26

1. Take days to repent (40—Jonah 3:4)	40
2. Add Josiah's age (8—2 Kings 22:1)	48
3. Divide by cities of refuge (6—Numbers 35:13)	8
4. Subtract the number of spies (2—Joshua 2:1)	6
5. Add pieces of silver (20—Genesis 37:28)	26

III. 9

1. Take the days Israelites wept (30—Deuteronomy 34:8)	30
2. Add the fish in the net (153—John 21:11)	183
3. Divide by times Elijah lay on the child (3—1 Kings 17:21)	61
4. Subtract the green withs (7—Judges 16:7)	54
5. Divide by the height of Goliath (6—1 Samuel 17:4)	9

IV. 175

1. Take horsemen sent to guard Paul (70—Acts 23:23)	70
2. Multiply by lepers (4—2 Kings 7:3)	280
3. Subtract height of ark (30—Genesis 6:15)	250
4. Divide by the righteous not found (10—Genesis 18:32)	25
5. Multiply by the days Job's friends tarried (7—Job 2:13)	175

V. 186

1. Take the years of the captivity (70—Jeremiah 25:11)   70
2. Multiply by the years Jacob served (6—Genesis 31:41)   420
3. Add number of generations (14—Matthew 1:17)   434
4. Divide by the times Naaman washed (7—2 Kings 5:10)   62
5. Multiply by the branches on vine (3—Genesis 40:10)   186

VI. 49

1. Take the number of stones (12—Joshua 4:3)   12
2. Times degrees backward (10—2 Kings 20:11)   120
3. Add the men in the boat (276—Acts 27:37)   396
4. Divide by steps on throne (6—1 Kings 10:19)   66
5. Less Jacob's years in Egypt (17—Genesis 47:28)   49

VII. 6

1. Take arrows shot toward David (3—1 Samuel 20:20)   3
2. Multiply by number of pots (6—John 2:6)   18
3. Divide by men who carried grapes (2—Numbers 13:23)   9
4. Add days in the grave (4—John 11:17)   13
5. Less number of times around Jericho (7—Joshua 6:15)   6

VIII. 1,312

1. Take beast's number (666—Revelation 13:18)   666
2. Divide by number of chains (2—Acts 12:6)   333
3. Subtract length of bed (9—Deuteronomy 3:11)   324
4. Add number of lords (1,000—Daniel 5:1)   1, 324
5. Less sons Jacob had (12—Genesis 35:22)   1,312

IX. 85

1. Take men sent for Jeremiah (30—Jeremiah 38:10)   30
2. Add Joseph's age (110—Genesis 50:26)   140
3. Less height of gallows (50—Esther 5:14)   90
4. Divide by measures of barley (6—Ruth 3:15)   15
5. Add years Tyre was forgotten (70—Isaiah 23:15)   85

X. 34

1. Take the prophets slain (450—1 Kings 18:22)   450
2. Divide by loaves (5—John 6:9)   90
3. Add number in Gideon's band (300—Judges 7:8)   390
4. Subtract age not reached (50—John 8:57)   340
5. Divide by sons of Haman (10—Esther 9:10)   34

XI. 11

1. Take number of stars (11—Genesis 37:9)   11
2. Multiply by porches (5—John 5:2)   55
3. Add years added (15—2 Kings 20:6)   70
4. Divide by stones (5—1 Samuel 17:40)   14
5. Subtract days without sight (3—Acts 9:9)   11

XII. 18

1. Numbers of days hiding (3—Joshua 2:16)   3
2. Multiply barrels of water (12—1 Kings 18:33-34)   36
3. Subtract days with Peter (15—Galatians 1:18)   21
4. Add furlongs distant (15—John 11:18)   36
5. Divide by Laban's daughters (2—Genesis 29:16)   18

Would You Believe It?

This is a very unusual quiz based upon the many strange facts found in the Bible. The purpose is to encourage the use of the Bible in finding the answers, since not many of them will be known from memory. The questions may be duplicated and given out one week, with the answers given the following week, allowing time for the students to search for the answers in their Bibles. Or they may be distributed in the Sunday school or morning service, and the answers given in the evening service. The quiz arouses a lot of curiosity and interest, and it encourages the use of the Bible concordance and dictionary in finding the answers. The questions are grouped in sets of ten, using such common themes as food, birds, insects, and kings.

I. BIBLE FOOD

1. What king fed seventy kings under his table? (Adoni-bezek—Judges 1:7)

2. What woman gave a king a gift of one hundred clusters of raisins? (Abigail to David—1 Samuel 25:18)

3. Who mentioned the white of an egg? (Job—Job 6:6)

4. Who went down into a garden of nuts? (Solomon—Song of Solomon 6:11)

5. Who was put on a diet for the rest of his life? (Jehoiachin—Jeremiah 52:34)

6. Who fed a hundred prophets in a cave with bread and water? (Obadiah—1 Kings 18:4)

7. Who was left as a lodge in a garden of cucumbers? (Israel, daughter of Zion—Isaiah 1:8)

8. Who made cakes to the queen of heaven? (Women of Jerusalem—Jeremiah 7:18)

9. Who was threatened with meat until it came out of their nostrils? (Israel—Numbers 11:18-20)

10. Who gave goat's broth to an angel? (Gideon—Judges 6: 11, 19)

II. BIBLE HOUSEHOLD

1. Where in the Bible does it tell how a man wipes dishes?
   (2 Kings 21:13—Wiping it, turning it upside down)

2. Who washed his steps with butter? (Job—Job 29:6)

3. What woman opened a bottle of milk to feed a captain?
   (Jael—Judges 4:19)

4. Who had a set of dishes made of pure gold? (Solomon—
   1 Kings 10:21)

5. Who ate the meat baked in the oven and dressed in the
   frying pan? (The priests—Leviticus 7:9)

6. Who spoke of washing with snow water? (Job—Job 9:30)

7. Where are short beds and narrow sheets mentioned?
   (Isaiah 28:20)

8. Whose bedroom had a floor of red, blue, white, and black
   marble? (Ahasuerus—Esther 1:6)

9. Who slept on a bed over thirteen feet long? (Og—Deuteronomy 3:11)

10. Who asked God to put his tears into a bottle? (David—
    Psalm 56:8)

III. BIBLE KINGS

1. What king reigned seven days and burned to death? (Zimri—1 Kings 16:15-18)

2. What dead king was laid on a bed filled with spices? (Asa—2 Chronicles 16:13-14)

3. What king brought water into a city? (Hezekiah—2 Kings 20:20)

4. What king was displeased with a present of twenty cities? (Hiram—1 Kings 9:11-13)

5. What king had a throne of ivory overlaid with gold? (Solomon—1 Kings 10:18)

6. What king had 900 chariots of iron? (Jabin—Judges 4:2-3)

7. What king sent presents carried by forty camels to a prophet? (Benhadad—2 Kings 8:7-9)

8. Where does it tell of seventy kings whose thumbs and toes were cut off? (Judges 1:7)

9. What king made himself a house of ivory? (Ahab—1 Kings 22:39)

10. What diseased king had to dwell in a separate house? (Uzziah—2 Kings 15:5; 2 Chronicles 26:21)

IV. BIBLE ANIMALS

1. How many horses were brought back from Babylon? (736—Nehemiah 7:68)

2. What price did Solomon pay for horses from Egypt? (150 shekels of silver—2 Chronicles 1:16-17)

3. When was an ox to be stoned to death? (When it gored a man or a woman—Exodus 21:28)

4. Who had thirty sons who rode on thirty ass colts? (Jair—Judges 10:3-4)

5. Where does it say the camels wore neckbands? (Judges 8:21, 26)

6. When was an ass's head sold for eighty pieces of silver? (Siege of Samaria—2 Kings 6:25)

7. From what animal's jawbone came forth water? (Ass's—Judges 15:15-19)

8. What nation had horses swifter than leopards? (Chaldeans—Habakkuk 1:6, 8)

9. Who saw a man riding a red horse at night? (Zechariah—Zechariah 1:8)

10. Who kept even the dogs from barking? (God—Exodus 11:7)

V. BIBLE CLOTHING

1. Where is a woman forbidden to wear a man's clothing? (Deuteronomy 22:5)

2. What two materials were forbidden in the same garment? (Wool and linen—Deuteronomy 22:11)

3. What fruit adorned the high priest's garment? (Pomegranates—Exodus 28:33)

4. What king died with a bracelet on his arm? (Saul—2 Samuel 1:10)

5. Who tore his new garment into twelve pieces? (Ahijah—1 Kings 11:30)

6. Who were sentenced to death with their hats on? (Shadrach, Meshach, and Abednego—Daniel 3:20-21)

7. Of what material were the first garments made? (Fig leaves—Genesis 3:7)

8. Who took off his shoe as a pledge of promise? (Boaz—Ruth 4:7-9)

9. Whose shoes did not wear out for forty years? (Israelites—Deuteronomy 29:5)

10. Who asked for two changes of garments and got leprosy? (Gehazi—2 Kings 5:22-27)

VI. BIBLE BIRDS

1. What bird makes its nest among the stars? (Eagle—Obadiah 1:4)

2. Where are four-footed fowls forbidden as food? (Leviticus 11:20)

3. Where does it say the stork makes her home? (Fir trees—Psalm 104:17)

4. Who spoke about a hen and her chickens? (Jesus—Matthew 23:37; Luke 13:34)

5. Where does it mention the sole of a dove's foot? (Genesis 8:9)

6. At what time of the year is the voice of the turtle dove heard? (Spring—Song of Solomon 2:11-12)

7. What bird bears her young on her wings? (Eagle—Deuteronomy 32:11)

8. What king grew hair like eagle's feathers? (Nebuchadnezzar—Daniel 4:33)

9. What prophet was brought his food by the ravens? (Elijah—1 Kings 17:6)

10. Who were told to be harmless as doves? (Disciples—Matthew 10:5, 16)

VII. BIBLE ANGELS

1. Who was struck on his side by an angel? (Peter—Acts 12: 7)

2. Who told angels to bathe their feet? (Abraham and Lot— Genesis 18:4; 19:1-2)

3. Where is angels' food mentioned in the Bible? (Psalm 78:24-25)

4. What angel argued with the devil over a man's body? (Michael—Jude 9)

5. What soldiers were frightened by an angel? (Guards at the tomb—Matthew 28:2-4)

6. What old man prepared food for angels? (Abraham— Genesis 18:1-22)

7. What animal saw an angel of the Lord? (Balaam's ass— Numbers 22:23)

8. Who was the angel that told a mother her baby's name? (Gabriel—Luke 1:26-31)

9. Who quoted the Bible verse about angels keeping charge over believers? (The devil—Matthew 4:6)

10. Who said the angel of the Lord kept him from the beasts? (Daniel—Daniel 6:22)

VIII. BIBLE WOMEN

1. What book of the Bible was written to a lady and her children? (2 John—2 John 1)

2. Who was the only woman whose age is mentioned in the Bible? (Sarah—Genesis 17:17; 23:1)

3. What woman lied to her father to spare her husband? (Michal—1 Samuel 19:12-17)

4. Who lost his wife to his best friend? (Samson—Judges 14:20)

5. Who had seven daughters to water his flocks? (Reuel—Exodus 2:16-18)

6. Whose skull was broken by a piece of a millstone cast down by a woman? (Abimelech's—Judges 9:53)

7. What woman gave birth to a child after she was ninety years old? (Sarah—Genesis 17:17; 21:1-2)

8. In what city did Tryphena and Tryphosa live? (Rome—Romans 16:12)

9. What two women in the church at Philippi were at odds? (Euodias and Syntyche—Philippians 4:2)

10. What five women demanded their rights to an inheritance? (Daughters of Zelophehad—Joshua 17:3-4)

IX. BIBLE ATHLETICS

1. What man was known for his furious driving? (Jehu—2 Kings 9:20)

2. What tribe had 700 expert left-handed stone-slingers? (Benjamin—Judges 20:15-16)

3. Who likened children to arrows, and a family to a quiver? (Psalmist—Psalm 127:4-5)

4. Who was a mighty hunter before the Lord? (Nimrod—Genesis 10:8-9)

5. Who drew in the net with 153 fishes? (Peter—John 21:11)

6. What twin was a cunning hunter, a man of the field? (Esau—Genesis 25:25, 27)

7. Who wrestled all night with God? (Jacob—Genesis 32:24-30)

8. Who warned that God would take them away with fish-hooks? (Amos—Amos 4:2)

9. Where are we admonished to run the race with patience? (Hebrews 12:1)

10. Where does it speak of hunting partridge in the mountains? (1 Samuel 26:20)

X. BIBLE OCCUPATIONS

1. What family was known for its horse-trading? (House of Togarmah—Ezekiel 27:14)

2. Who had his wages changed ten times? (Jacob—Genesis 31:4-7)

3. What preacher worked at the craft of tent-making? (Paul—Acts 18:1-3)

4. What were the occupations of Joseph's two fellow prisoners? (Butler and baker—Genesis 40:1-3)

5. Who was the lawyer for whom Paul sent? (Zenas—Titus 3:13)

6. Who was the first shepherd mentioned in the Bible? (Abel—Genesis 4:2)

7. Who built the first city and named it after his son? (Cain—Genesis 4:17)

8. Who served as secretary to the prophet Jeremiah? (Baruch—Jeremiah 36:4)

9. Who earned his living as a gatherer of sycamore fruit? (Amos—Amos 7:14)

10. What did Haggai say was wrong with the wage earner's purse? (It had holes in it—Haggai 1:6)

XI. BIBLE MARRIAGE

1. Who said "Whoso findeth a wife findeth a good thing"? (Solomon—Proverbs 18:22)

2. What Hebrew lad married the daughter of an Egyptian priest? (Joseph—Genesis 41:45)

3. What men passed off their wives as their sisters? (Abraham and Isaac—Genesis 12:10-20; 20:1-18; 26:6-16)

4. Who referred to his wife as a heifer? (Samson—Judges 14:18)

5. Who objected to Moses' marriage to an Ethiopian? (Miriam and Aaron—Numbers 12:1)

6. Who was the first bigamist? (Lamech—Genesis 4:19)

7. Who called her husband a bloody man? (Zipporah—Exodus 4:25)

8. Who worked seven years for a wife and got her sister instead? (Jacob—Genesis 29:16-26)

9. Who slew 200 men to get his wife? (David—1 Samuel 18:27)

10. What wife put a dummy in a bed to represent her husband? (Michal—1 Samuel 19:13-16)

XII. BIBLE CHILDREN

1. Who kidnapped a little boy and hid him for seven years? (Jehosheba—2 Kings 11:1-21)

2. Who cursed little children when called "bald head"? (Elisha—2 Kings 2:23-24)

3. What adopted daughter became the queen of Persia? (Esther—Esther 2:7)

4. Whose child sneezed seven times after being dead? (Shunamite woman's—2 Kings 4:32-36)

5. What father named a city for his son? (Cain—Genesis 4:17)

6. What three boys had a father 500 years old? (Shem, Ham, and Japheth—Genesis 5:32)

7. What amusement of little children is mentioned by Jesus? (Piping and dancing—Matthew 11:16-17)

8. What child was dropped by his nurse and became lame? (Mephibosheth—2 Samuel 4:4)

9. What son died from a sunstroke? (Son of the Shunamite woman—2 Kings 4:18-20)

10. Who named one of his daughters after a spice? (Job; he named her Kezia, or Cassia—Job 42:14)

XIII. BIBLE DEATHS

1. What man had his dwelling among the tombs of the dead? (Demoniac—Mark 5:2-3)

2. What men were buried in the same cave with their wives? (Abraham, Isaac and Jacob—Genesis 25:9-10; 49:28-33; 50:12-13)

3. Who put up his own tombstone as a remembrance? (Absalom—2 Samuel 18:18)

4. Who saw a valley full of dead men's bones? (Ezekiel—Ezekiel 37:1-14)

5. What maker of clothing was raised from the dead? (Dorcas—Acts 9:37-40)

6. Who was hanged on the gallows he prepared for another? (Haman—Esther 7:10)

7. Who fell off a seat backward and died of a broken neck? (Eli—1 Samuel 4:15, 18)

8. Who hanged himself because his advice was rejected? (Ahithophel—2 Samuel 17:23)

9. Whose bones were carried forty years through the wilderness? (Joseph's—Genesis 50:25-26; Exodus 13:19; Joshua 24:32)

10. Who was buried by God in a place no man knew? (Moses—Deuteronomy 34:5-6)

XIV. BIBLE EDUCATION

1. Who said, "Of making many books there is no end"? (Solomon—Ecclesiastes 12:12)

2. Where does it speak of musicians, teachers, and scholars casting lots for jobs? (1 Chronicles 25:8)

3. Who ordered his book to be cast into the river? (Jeremiah—Jeremiah 51:63)

4. Who said that he would not write with paper and ink? (John—2 John 1:12)

5. What is referred to as our schoolmaster? (The Law—Galatians 3:24)

6. Who called attention to his writing with large letters? (Paul—Galatians 6:11)

7. Where did foreigners outdo native students in intelligence? (Babylon—Daniel 1:19-20)

8. Who spoke of much study as a weariness of the flesh? (Solomon—Ecclesiastes 12:12)

9. Who warned against the dangers of philosophy? (Paul—Colossians 2:8)

10. Who wished his words were printed in a book? (Job—Job 19:23)

XV. BIBLE REFERENCES TO STRONG DRINK

1. Who was advised to drink a little wine for his infirmities? (Timothy—1 Timothy 5:23)

2. Who wished for his son plenty of corn and wine? (Isaac, for Jacob—Genesis 27:28)

3. Who spoke about garments being washed in wine? (Jacob—Genesis 49:1-2, 10-12)

4. Who was the first person the Bible tells about becoming drunk? (Noah—Genesis 9:20-21)

5. When were the disciples accused of being drunken? (At Pentecost—Acts 2:13)

6. Which king had a wine cellar in his home? (David— 1 Chronicles 27:27)

7. Who turned six waterpots of water into wine at a wedding? (Jesus—John 2:1-11)

8. Where does it say that wine bites like snakes? (Proverbs 23:32)

9. Where does it say the people sold a girl for wine to drink? (Joel 3:3)

10. Who drank wine in the sacred vessels from the Temple? (Belshazzur and others—Daniel 5:1-2)

XVI. BIBLE CITIES

1. What city was built with the sacrifice of two sons? (Jericho—1 Kings 16:34)

2. What city did the Lord come down from heaven to see? (Babel—Genesis 11:5-9)

3. What was the name of the first city ever built? (Enoch—Genesis 4:17)

4. Paul shook off the dust of his feet against what city? (Antioch in Pisidia—Acts 13:14-15, 50-51)

5. What is the only city to come down out of heaven? (New Jerusalem—Revelation 21:2)

6. From what city did Paul escape, being let down in a basket? (Damascus—Acts 9:22-25; 2 Corinthians 11:32-33)

7. What city was known as the city of palm trees? (Jericho—Deuteronomy 34:3)

8. What city was known for its fairs with horses and horsemen? (Tyre—Ezekiel 27:13-14)

9. What city was exalted to heaven? (Capernaum—Luke 10:15)

10. What city had 120,000 inhabitants who could not tell the right hand from the left? (Nineveh—Jonah 4:11)

XVII. BIBLE QUEENS

1. What queen forged the king's name on important papers? (Jezebel—1 Kings 21:7-8)

2. What queen's body was devoured by the dogs? (Jezebel's—2 Kings 9:30-36)

3. What queen was deposed for refusing the king's command? (Vashti—Esther 1:10-21)

4. What queen disguised herself to the prophet of God? (Wife of Jeroboam—1 Kings 14:2-6)

5. What queen requested a man's head on a platter? (Herodias—Mark 6:17-24)

6. What Jewish maiden became queen of Persia? (Esther—Esther 2:17)

7. What queen attempted to slay all her grandchildren? (Athaliah—2 Kings 11:1-3)

8. What queen exclaimed "The half was not told me"? (Queen of Sheba—1 Kings 10:7)

9. To what queen did the women of Jerusalem make cakes? (Queen of heaven—Jeremiah 7:18)

10. What queen's treasurer was converted while riding in a chariot? (Candace, queen of Ethiopia—Acts 8:27)

XVIII. BIBLE MITES

1. What two kings were forced to flee from hornets? (Sihon and Og—Joshua 24:12; 2:10)

2. Where is the bat mentioned in the Bible? (Leviticus 11: 19; Deuteronomy 14:18)

3. What prophet spoke of the plague of locusts? (Joel—Joel 1:4)

4. In what land did the dust turn into lice? (Egypt—Exodus 8:17)

5. Who found frogs in their beds and in their food? (Egyptians—Exodus 8:3, 6)

6. Who shall put his hand on a cockatrice's den? (A little child—Isaiah 11:8)

7. For what use was a chameleon forbidden? (For food—Leviticus 11:30)

8. Who builds his house as a moth? (The wicked—Job 27:18)

9. What insects were the common food of John the Baptist? (Locusts—Matthew 3:5)

10. Where does it speak of a king seeking a flea? (1 Samuel 26:20)